CHRIST OUR SURE FOUNDATION

Sermons For
Pentecost (First Third)
Cycle A, Gospel Texts

MARC KOLDEN

CSS Publishing Company, Inc.
Lima, Ohio

CHRIST OUR SURE FOUNDATION

Library of Congress Cataloging-in-Publication Data

Kolden, Marc.
Christ our sure foundation : sermons for Pentecost (first third) : Cycle A Gospel lesson texts / Marc Kolden.
p. cm.
ISBN 0-7880-0499-9
1. Pentecost season—Sermons 2. Sermons, English. 3. Bible. N.T. Gospels—Sermons. I. Title.
BV61.K648 1995
252'.67—dc20 95-14050
CIP

This book is available in the following formats, listed by ISBN:
0-7880-0499-9 Book
0-7880-0500-6 IBM 3 1/2 computer disk
0-7880-0501-4 IBM 3 1/2 book and disk package
0-7880-0502-2 Macintosh computer disk
0-7880-0503-0 Macintosh book and disk package
0-7880-0504-9 IBM 5 1/4 computer disk
0-7880-0505-7 IBM 5 1/4 book and disk package

PRINTED IN U.S.A.

In Memory of my Parents:

Osborne Kolden, 1912-1946

Jim Grier, 1906-1986

Eunice Lunde Kolden Grier, 1911-1993

Editor's Note Regarding The Lectionary

•Lectionary Uniformity

During the past two decades there has been an attempt to move in the direction of a uniform lectionary among various Protestant denominations.

•Christian Unity

Preaching on the same scripture lessons every Sunday is a step in the right direction of uniting Christians of many faiths. If we are reading the same scriptures together we may also begin to accomplish other achievements. Our efforts will be strengthened through our unity.

•ELCA Adopts Revised Common Lectionary

Beginning with Advent 1995 The Evangelical Lutheran Church in America will drop its own lectionary schedule and adopt the Revised Common Lectionary.

•For Those In Transition

We at CSS Publishing Company heartily embrace this change. We recognize, however, that there will be a transitional period during which some churches may continue for a time to use the traditional Lutheran lectionary. In order to accommodate these clergy and churches who may still be referring to the Lutheran lectionary we will for a period of time continue to provide sermons and illustrations based on scriptural passages from BOTH the Lutheran and The Revised Common lectionaries.

Table Of Contents

C — Revised Common Lectionary; L — Lutheran Lectionary; RC — Roman Catholic Lectionary

Preface

As a teacher who now sits in the pew at least half of the Sundays of each year, I have come to reflect on preaching not only from the point of view of the preacher but also from that of the hearer. The chief insight I have come to is that it is very easy *not* to hear the biblical passages that supposedly form the basis for the sermon. When that happens, even if the sermon is in fact rooted in and drawn from the biblical text, it is often difficult for the listener to see the connection.

This has led me to make a conscious strategic decision in writing these sermons *always* to begin by retelling the biblical story or even (in some cases) going through it in some detail, verse by verse. In this way, even if the hearer has tuned out during the reading of the lessons, the words of the sermon attempt to make sure that the hearer gets tuned in again to the words of scripture.

This means that none of the sermons starts with an example or a personal story. There are no communication gimmicks or rhetorical techniques used to hook the hearer. I have sought instead to depend on the message of the biblical passage itself (in this volume, the assigned gospel reading) to establish a connection to the hearer's mind and heart. You, the reader, will be the best judge of whether or not this happens. To no one's surprise, I suppose, those who know the Bible best and probably tune out the lessons least often appreciate these sorts of sermons the most. And that's fine. But my real reason for this approach is not only to reach but also to teach those who do not know the story very well.

In addition to this preaching strategy, there is a principled reason for beginning doggedly and consistently with retelling the biblical passage. It is this: the only excuse for speaking our words from the pulpit is that they are drawn from, dependent on and intended to convey the message of God's word. While human artistry, scholarship and insight are all important in preaching, it is not a Christian sermon if it does not proclaim God's word. And while God's word is not limited to what is written in the Bible, since Jesus Christ himself is the epitome of God's word according to the Bible itself, nevertheless the Bible is a source of our knowledge of Christ and must be allowed to have priority if we are to preach Christ rightly.

There is no explicit argument for the authority of scripture or theories of composition or inspiration contained in these sermons. I understand the authority of scripture to be primarily functional: it will have the authority God intends if in fact it is used to authorize our preaching and teaching. Thus I want to start with scripture — every time.

This is a matter of both form and content, although so far I have been emphasizing form. When scripture occupies such a central place in the sermon's form, however, it also tends to dominate its content. In part I have tried simply to draw the content of the sermons from the biblical passages themselves and then relate it to modern day disciples of Jesus. Yet it is never that simple. I write as a Christian committed to the classical creeds and dogmas of the one, holy, catholic and apostolic church as well as one who has been thoroughly shaped by the sixteenth century Reformation's emphases on Christ alone and faith alone.

Coming at the message of the Bible with such comments has led me to use (at least implicitly) two criteria to test each sermon: 1) Did Jesus have to die on the cross for this sermon to be preached? and 2) Does this sermon convey true comfort to real sinners? These criteria are part of a way of understanding the biblical message that, for me, is decisive. They also in the course of my ministry have forced me to do more rewriting than I care to remember! While these sermons may not in every case satisfy the criteria, doing so is my intention — and should be the intention of every preacher, I would agree.

The reader will notice that in many of the sermons, usually near the end, there is a section relating the message directly to the sacrament of Holy Communion. In the congregation of which I am a member, we have Holy Communion at one of the two services each Sunday morning but usually not at the other. That practice was on my mind as I prepared these sermons. Therefore, the short sections on Holy Communion are placed in brackets [ ], so they may be included or omitted as appropriate.

Finally, I have used several books on the gospel of Matthew (from which most of these sermons are drawn) and I wish to acknowledge my debt to their authors. I regularly consulted Eduard Schweizer, *The Good News According To Matthew* (Atlanta: John Knox Press, 1975). In addition, I continue to learn from an old book on discipleship by Martin Franzmann, *Follow Me: Discipleship According To Saint Matthew* (St. Louis: Concordia Publishing House, 1961). Above all I have benefitted from the marvelous book by Frederick Dale Bruner, *The Christbook: A Historical/Theological Commentary On Matthew 1-12* (Waco, Texas: Word Books, 1987). Professor Bruner, of Whitworth College, Spokane, Washington, has combined not only acute biblical, historical, and theological insights into a most readable work, but he has reached a depth of spiritual and missionary understanding that is most remarkable. Reading the book was a deeply moving faith experience for me and I was tempted in many instances to lift portions of it directly into my sermons. While I trust that I have not plagiarized his work, I want to express my great thanks to Professor Bruner. I would encourage all preachers on Matthew to use this book. (There is also a second volume by Bruner, *The Churchbook*, which deals with Matthew 13-28.)

This book is dedicated to my parents. I have had three parents: one mother and two fathers. My birth father, Osborne Kolden, died when I was six but had already been a major influence in my life, not least of all through his Christian faith. My stepfather, Jim Grier, married my mother when I was nine and was my father until he died 37 years later. My mother, Eunice (Lunde), died during the year in which these sermons were written. In fact, my brothers and I cleaned out the old family home in northern Minnesota and ordered the gravestone for my mother and stepfather a week before I sent in the manuscript. They are buried together in the woods behind the house. They died, as they lived, with Christ. For that, and for a lot of other blessings from all three of these parents, I am thankful.

Marc Kolden

Pentecost
John 20:19-23

The Breath Of God

Pentecost is the third great Christian festival. On Christmas we celebrated the birth of Christ, our Savior. On Easter we celebrated his victorious resurrection from death. And today we remember Christ's giving of the Holy Spirit.

Our story from the gospel of John takes place on Easter evening, after the disciples had discovered that the tomb was empty and Jesus had appeared to Mary Magdalene. Jesus told her to tell the disciples that he was risen, which she did, but they did not understand. So on that first evening they were gathered in a house with the doors locked, because they were afraid — afraid of being killed, just as Jesus had been killed three days before. But suddenly Jesus was among them and he said, "Peace be with you."

"Peace be with you." A greeting, yes, but not just, "Hi, how are you?" "Peace" is a huge biblical word. It refers to a wholeness, a completeness, a divine healing that envelopes people. It is a "peace that passes human understanding" (Philippians 4:7); it is "peace, not as the world gives" (John 14:27) — not merely a lessening of conflict; not just a momentary break in the action — but the great relief and security and hopefulness that comes from being in the presence of the

God of love. To this scared group of former followers, the risen Christ begins by bringing the peace of God.

Jesus said it twice; did you notice? "Peace be with you." We are not to miss it. And in between his speaking, he showed them the marks in his hands and sides, which he had suffered on the cross. Then it began to dawn on them. This was really Jesus, who had been crucified, who had died on the cross, but now he was alive. And it says that the disciples "rejoiced" when they saw "the Lord." Their lives were changed from disabling fear into joy by the presence of the risen Lord.

"Lord" in the Bible is also a huge word. Here it does not mean only "Master" or "leader." It is one of the Old Testament's names for God, after all. To say that the disciples saw "the Lord" is to report that they saw one who was not only their friend and companion and leader but was truly the one sent from God. They had hoped that this was true; they had stuck their necks out to follow him and be his disciples. But when he had been put to death on the cross as a common criminal, their hopes had faltered; fear had replaced faith and sorrow had banished hope. Now Jesus' coming into their midst as Lord, bringing the peace of God, reversed all that.

We might think that this was the climax, but actually it was only the beginning. "Peace be with you" is just the first sentence. Then Jesus continues, "As the Father has sent me, so I send you." God the Father sent the only Son from heaven to save the world and now that Son says, "That's how I'm now sending you." Can you imagine those disciples? Here they were, huddled in fear, hiding in a house with locked doors, just trying to save their own skins. And Jesus comes and says he is sending *them* to save the world. What a turn of events. The disciples were on the defensive; now Jesus sends them out on offense.

Defensive driving is a good idea. An attorney for the defense is important. In sports a good defense is essential. But defensive Christianity is not a biblical idea. The posture of Christian disciples is not hiding in fear trying to protect themselves. No, disciples are *sent*. There may still be reason to fear; there may still be confusion. After all, if disciples are sent in the same way that Jesus was sent, that could be very frightening. But to be a follower of Jesus after his resurrection is to be sent. In fact, our word "apostle" means "one who is sent."

Like "peace" and "Lord," "send" is also a huge biblical word. In Saint John's gospel it is used over and over about Jesus, the one whom God sent to save the world. When Jesus tells his followers that they are now being sent, this is a divine commission: *God* is sending them. That's why they were called and gathered in the first place: in order to be sent.

It's a bit like the military: basic training isn't an end in itself; it is for the sake of carrying out future missions. It's like being on an athletic team: practice is not the real thing; it's preparation for the real thing, the game. So too, as Christians, when we gather for worship and study, prayer and praise, these are not all there is to being Christ's followers. We too are sent. If this sounds like more than we bargained for, then we need to be sure to hear the rest of this passage.

After Jesus had told them that he was sending them, it says that he "breathed on them." Now if you have heard even a few Bible stories, those words should be familiar. In the book of Genesis, in the story of God forming the first human beings from the dust of the earth, it says he "breathed into his nostrils the breath of life" (Genesis 2:7). In Psalm 104:29-30, it says that when you, God, take away creatures' breath, they die and return to dust, but "when you send forth your spirit [or breath! They are the same word], they are created." Jesus breathed on those disciples and if that was not plain enough, his words told them what it means: "Receive the Holy Spirit." "Receive the breath of God." In that moment, the risen Christ raised those fearful, faithless followers to newness of life.

This is what Pentecost is: the giving of the Spirit, the giving of new life, from the Father through the Son. The Holy Spirit is what makes it possible for people to go when they are sent. The Spirit is God's active, personal presence that accompanies those who are sent. And the Spirit brings the content and the power for the task for which Christ's followers are sent. Jesus says, "Receive the Holy Spirit. Go and forgive sins." That's what being gathered is all about: that the followers may be forgiven and renewed, sent and equipped, in order that all people may be reconciled to God by having their sins forgiven.

Sin is the problem. Forgiveness is the solution. Sin means that we are enemies of God, that things are not right between us, that we have gone astray, that we do not trust the one who made us in the first place. Forgiveness of sins on account of Christ means that while we were God's enemies, God took it upon himself to wipe away our wrongdoings and our guilt and make us friends. Forgiveness of sins means that God seeks the lost, welcomes back the prodigal, binds up the poor and brokenhearted. Forgiveness of sins means that God in Christ proves to be trustworthy by never letting go of us, so that we can trust again. Jesus sends his followers with the gift of the Holy Spirit to save the world by forgiving sins.

He really seems to be taking a chance by doing it this way. "If you forgive the sins of any, they are forgiven them; if you retain the sins of any, they are retained." God acts now through those who follow Jesus: they (we!) must pronounce the words of forgiveness if people are to be forgiven. And if they (we) do not do so, if they (we) retain the sins of some, those people will not be forgiven. Heavy words. A lot like, "As the Father has sent me, so I send you."

Some Christian groups have applied these words about our forgiving sins only to the original twelve disciples or (more commonly) only to ordained ministers. But neither here in John's gospel nor in other places (for example, Matthew 18:18, Luke 24:33, 47) is it clear that only some Christians are to speak words of forgiveness. John commonly distinguishes between "the twelves" and a larger group of disciples; "disciple" is more of a generic term for any and all who followed Christ and it is to disciples that Jesus speaks in our passage today.

Just as the promise in the Old Testament was that the Spirit one day would be poured out on "all flesh" (Joel 2:28), and just as the New Testament teaches that no one could believe if not for the Holy Spirit (Romans 8:9-17, indicating that all Christians receive the Holy Spirit), so also we need to realize that the command to forgive sins applies to all of us. It simply means that we are all to share the Gospel: as we do it, people will hear and believe; as we do not do it, they will not hear and believe but will remain lost in their sins. That is the risk God takes in Christ.

That's why it is so important that we hear this story today so that through it Jesus can give us peace. We need to hear the story so that Jesus can remind us again that he is sending us to proclaim the Gospel of the forgiveness of sins. We need to know that through his word he again breathes the Holy Spirit, the breath of God, on us — recreating us as individuals and as a holy people, as his very own body, the church. Pentecost was the day that the church was born. The Spirit was given then. But that wasn't the end of it. That was only the beginning. The mission goes on as God's Spirit today bestows Christ's peace, forgives sins and draws people together in Jesus' name.

[As the capstone of the Spirit's work today we are offered Christ himself, his own body and blood, so that we might *be* his body in the world: "the forgiven," as someone has said, "learning to forgive." Before we eat the bread and drink from the cup, we will echo Jesus' words, "Peace be with you." For us also it is not merely a casual greeting but a concrete bestowal of the gift of divine peace that comes from Christ to our neighbor through us. God has already begun to equip us to go out forgiving sins by allowing us to be vessels of divine grace at this worship service.]

Each one of us has life only by the constant gift of God's breath of life. Each of us has faith in Jesus Christ and hope for eternal life only by the ongoing work of God's Spirit through the means of grace. Each of us, by the gift of that Spirit, is a disciple of Jesus Christ sent forth in God's world in the company of the faithful.

The Spirit of God, the breath of God, the divine wind that blows where God wills, blows into our bodies in every moment, keeping us alive; it blows into our hearts and minds and souls, bringing us faith and new life; and it brings us the peace of God and sends us out — blows us out, really — where we will be swept up in the marvelous saving work of God.

Go in peace. Serve the Lord.

Holy Trinity
Matthew 28:16-20

God Deep In The Flesh

Our gospel reading today from Matthew 28 is both famous and familiar. Most of us have heard it many times. It is Jesus' "Great Commission" to the eleven disciples shortly after his resurrection. The disciples go to the mountaintop and the risen Christ comes to them in the midst of their doubts and astonishment and speaks those amazing words: "All authority in heaven and on earth has been given to me." What an incredible claim! But here, of course, the point is that it is the one to whom all authority has been given who then tells the disciples what they are to do. So we had better listen.

"Go therefore and make disciples of all nations." Gather more followers, call more people to faith — people of every class and background, of every land and race — for Jesus is the Lord of the whole world, after all. "Baptizing them in the name of the Father and of the Son and of the Holy Spirit." That is, join them to Christ by washing away their sins and calling them to repentance and faith and to unity with all believers in Christ's body, the church. "Teaching them to obey everything I have commanded you." To be a disciple, to be a baptized member of Christ's body, is to follow Jesus, to live by his teachings, to serve in his mission, to pray for his kingdom. This is a radically new way of life, for us as it once was for those first disciples. People have to be taught, shown, led, and encouraged if they are to be disciples. This is an integral part of the Christian mission.

Then comes the conclusion, the powerful promise that undergirds the receiving of this Great Commission. "And remember, I am with you always, to the end of the age." That's the key — for us as for those first disciples. Not only does Jesus have all authority; not only does he send his followers out; but, above all, he promises always to be present. Nothing in the Christian mission would work without Christ's presence. And this brings us to the heart of the matter of this Trinity Sunday. This is the Sunday on which we focus on the total reality of God — Father, Son, and Holy Spirit. The triune God is the one in whose name we are baptized and in whose name we gather for worship and on whose mission Christ sends us and on whose *being* Christ's promise to be always present depends.

The doctrine of the Trinity is not primarily about numbers, even though it says that God is one divine nature in three persons. Rather, the doctrine of the Trinity is about *who* God is. We might say that "Father, Son, and Holy Spirit" is the "brand name" of God. Often, it seems, we think of God in generic terms. Everybody knows what God is, we say: God is a being who is powerful, transcendent, perhaps wrathful or judgmental, holy and unchanging, and so forth. Such a generic God is regularly invoked by everyone from politicians to witnesses in a courtroom, from those reciting the pledge of allegiance to those using profanity, from our response to someone who sneezes to the subject of highly abstract philosophical speculation. But such a god "up there" somewhere, largely unknown and increasingly irrelevant, is quite unlike the God of the Bible, the God whom we know above all in Jesus Christ.

Someone has helpfully said that our God is best thought of as a God who is "deep in the flesh." That's what the doctrine of the Trinity is about: God deep in the flesh. That's why on this Trinity Sunday we worship God by listening to the words of the one in whom God became flesh, Jesus Christ. Here we have a picture of God as anything but remote or irrelevant. Here we have God deep in the flesh of history and matter, of life and death, of grief and joy.

It is Jesus in whom God is truly defined and identified. The only reason Christians even talk about God as three-in-one is because of Jesus. It is because Jesus came and proclaimed God's kingdom and spoke with divine authority and forgave sins and cast out evil spirits and healed the sick; it is because Jesus called into question the religion of his time and the rulers of his age and was executed on a cross; and it is because this crucified one was raised from the dead that Christians have had to find a way to speak of God that includes Jesus. If it hadn't been that people found that they encountered the true God when they met Jesus no one would ever have thought of speaking of God as a trinity. But if there can only be one God, one who is ultimate and above all others, and yet we experience meeting the one God in the human Jesus and in the Spirit who is given after Jesus' resurrection to draw us to him, then we must talk about this one God in a way that includes Jesus and the Spirit.

The reformer Martin Luther once said that we should never say anything about God that we cannot say about the man Jesus Christ. He said that we should not speak about God as immortal or omnipotent or by using most of the other classical attributes of God. Why? Because even though such things may be true, they are so far above us that we cannot know for sure. What we can be sure about God is what we know in Jesus — that God is loving, forgiving, merciful, and faithful; that God came to seek and save the lost; that God hates sin and injustice; and yet that God is a friend of sinners and suffers and dies to bring them to salvation. Luther's point is that we should speak about God by speaking about Jesus, because Jesus is God deep in the flesh. The Bible calls Jesus the visible image of the invisible God (Colossians 1:15) and someone in our day has referred to Jesus as "the human face of

God.'' When we want to know who the true God is, we look to Jesus. That's what the doctrine of the Trinity is all about — that we only speak of the true God when we speak of the relation of the Father and the Son and of the bond or spirit between them.

Some people have worried recently about using male language such as Father and Son in speaking of God. Doesn't that seem to exclude women? Doesn't it suggest that God is male (or, worse, several males)? That certainly can be a problem if we don't remember what the doctrine of the Trinity is really about — and it is not about God's being a male. The Bible does not attribute sexuality to God — and in that it is very different from other ancient religions. Instead, the doctrine of the Trinity is about the *close relationship* of the historical person Jesus to the divine reality. This is portrayed in the New Testament by the very familiar language of parent and child, in this case, father and son. The main point of the image is not its maleness but its closeness, its intimacy. The Bible is showing us that the God whom Jesus addressed as ''father'' is as close to him as a loving parent is close to a beloved child.

The point for faith of this intimate relationship is that Jesus speaks for God, that God speaks and acts in Jesus, that faith in Jesus *is* faith in the true God. The point of the doctrine of the Trinity for faith is that when Jesus died for our sins, *God* indeed acted for our salvation. The point for faith is that in Jesus' name we too can approach God as our father, as Jesus directs us in the Lord's prayer. It is important to remember that the church has never claimed that it is Jesus' maleness that is important in the incarnation; it is his *humanness* that is essential. In Christ, we believe, God took our human nature into the divine life. So today we need to be careful that when we speak of Father, Son and Holy Spirit we do so because that is the way that we clearly identify God as the God who saves us in Jesus (that is what is essential). But we must not use that triune identity in ways that would denigrate or exclude women either in their relation to God or in their roles in God's world.

Speaking of the triune God in this way, with the central focus on Jesus so that we have a God that we know we can trust for salvation, may seem to some of you to be too narrowly related only to religion or to eternal life. In fact, our passage from Matthew 28 may itself seem too narrow if it relates the triune God only to our going out and making disciples. Is that all that Christianity is about? Are we all supposed to be evangelists? What about work and family and school and politics and the environment? What about the needs of this life and its trials and griefs, its joys and victories? Is Christianity only about some future life and not this one?

In fact, I think we must say that we are all supposed to be evangelists. Making disciples is the chief calling of all Christians, according to the New Testament. But that doesn't mean that Christianity is only about some other life in the future. Precisely being a disciple of the triune God has everything to do with work and family and school and politics and the environment as well as the griefs and joys of this present life. This is the case because belief in the triune God means that the God who creates and the God who saves and the God who will raise us to eternal life is *one* God. Salvation in Jesus is not an escape from this world but a reclamation and renewal of the created world. Jesus came, after all, because God loved the world. Jesus the Savior was involved in the creation of the world (John 1; Colossians 1), just as the sanctifying Spirit is portrayed also as the creating Spirit (Genesis 1; Psalm 104).

We must not pit religion and life against each other if we believe in the triune God. In the Bible, redemption is for the sake of creation; the church is for the sake of the world; faith is to lead to earthly works. Christians are called not to be spiritual virtuosos but to be faithful *creatures*. Some Christians all through history have gotten this wrong. They have argued that the creator God is not the Father of Jesus Christ but some alien being; they have believed that the Holy Spirit who gives spiritual gifts is not the same as the Spirit who gives life.

The doctrine of the Trinity was formulated against such misunderstandings in its insistence that the Father, the Son, and the Spirit are one, sharing in one divine nature. This means that in the Incarnation God is not doing something totally different but rather something totally in keeping with the creation of all things in the first place. And this means that we Christians, when we are called to be disciples and to make disciples, are not called out of the world but more deeply back into it, because the world belongs to God and is the place of God's ongoing creating and redeeming activity.

Believing in the God who is deep in the flesh of Jesus Christ reveals to us a God who has always been creating and preserving and rescuing flesh and blood. When the Bible speaks of Christ Jesus "emptying himself" (Philippians 2:6-8) this is right in keeping with the way that God has poured out love in making us in the divine image and in breathing life into us and in being faithful to us and to all people in ways that surpass all human understanding. This shouldn't be a strange idea to us who expect to hear God's Word from human speakers, who regularly see God acting through word and water in baptism, who believe that as we eat the bread and drink the wine of the Lord's supper that we receive Christ himself, and who have been praying since long before we ever heard the word "trinity" to a God we address as "our father." Trinity Sunday is a time for seeing how our Christian faith and practice fit with the reality of God.

Being a disciple of Jesus means following in this way of embracing the world and its people and its challenges and its joys precisely because it is here that we meet the one who promises to be with us always. Of course, the world is messed up by sin, just as each one of us is; of course, the ways of this sinful world are not God's ways. But the way of discipleship, the way of the triune God, is not away *from* the world and sinners but *to* it and *for* them, with a message of good news — of forgiveness and new life, of hope and purpose, of a calling to be Christ's disciples.

Notice that after the resurrection Jesus did not begin by calling all new people, despite the fact that the original disciples had all forsaken him at the crucifixion. Rather, he recalled these same people, forgave them, and sent them out. That must have shocked them almost as much as others who found out about it. But for them and for us it is the wonderful news that we aren't saved by what we do but solely by grace through faith (Ephesians 2:8-9).

The risen Lord who originally spoke the words written in Matthew 28 is present here today, calling us to join the eleven in being his disciples and sending us out from here to live as disciples and to invite others into life with God. It says we are to "make disciples," but I think all of us know that we by ourselves don't really do that. We tell the story; we live the faith; but it is God's own Spirit who actually makes disciples. Without the Spirit, scripture says, we couldn't even pray, let alone say that "Jesus is Lord" (Romans 8:26, 1 Corinthians 12:3). God's Spirit makes believers out of us. That's a promise. From the Father, through the Son. Thanks be to God! Amen.

Proper 4
Pentecost 2
Ordinary Time 9
Matthew 7:21-29 (C)
Matthew 7:(15-20) 21-29 (L)
Matthew 7:21-27 (RC)

The Sure Foundation

Today we have heard two short sayings from the very end of Jesus' Sermon on the Mount. First Jesus says, "Not everyone who says, 'Lord, Lord,' will enter the kingdom of heaven." Not everyone who says, "I believe"; not all who say they are Christians; not everyone who claims to have done great deeds in Christ's name will be saved. "But only the one who does the will of my Father in heaven." And we say, "Oh, my. Does that mean me? Am I one of those who is all talk and no walk?"

Then Jesus speaks of those who hear his words and act on them as being like the wise man who built his house on a solid rock foundation, where the storms could not move it. But he adds a warning about those who hear his words but do not act on them; he says they are like the foolish man who set his house on sand and it was toppled when the storms came. And again, this may hit pretty close to home. We wonder, "Am I one of those whose life is built on sand? Will I be swept away by the storms of God's judgment?"

These two sayings of Jesus are directed to those of us who are Christians. We, not non-Christians, are the ones who are prone to be more concerned about believing than doing, about words than about deeds. The first saying (about those who say, "Lord, Lord") is directed especially against those of us who are pastors and teachers and leaders in the Christian community, who speak a lot about Christ and represent him publicly. Such persons, above all, have to ask, do our lives fit with what we say? The second saying of Jesus, about where we build our houses, applies to all Christians: "Everyone who hears these words of mine" and does or does not act on them. The house (or the life) that falls is the house of persons who find Jesus' words important enough to hear but not realistic enough to live.

When we remember that these words conclude all the exhortations and warnings of the Sermon on the Mount in Matthew 5-7, we cannot help but feel their heavy weight. We must do the will of God or we will be cast out; we must hear Jesus' words and do them or we will fall. This does not sound like good news. Yet it is the word of God for us this day and we dare not simply reject it because it makes us feel afraid or guilty. So we must look closely at these words — in terms of their context, in terms of who said them, and in terms of their specific content.

It makes all the difference in the world who says something. If the President of the United States says something, it has much more weight than if an anonymous radio talk-show caller says the same thing. If a person of color speaks words about being free, we hear them differently than if they are spoken by a white person. If a woman reads the words of Galatians 3:27-28 about in Christ there is no longer Jew or Greek, no longer slave or free, no longer male and female, we hear this passage in a different way than if a man reads it.

The one who speaks the words of our gospel passage today is the one who has called us to follow him, just as he called the original disciples, and who began this Sermon on the Mount with a series of blessings that we call the Beatitudes. More than that, the Jesus who speaks these words is the one whom scripture calls "Emmanuel," God with us, the one who was sent to *save* his people, not to cast them out.

Jesus' words are far more than only a list of demands or warnings. He came to reclaim people, not to drive them away. He came to shape us into his image, to change us, not to lose us. He came to mold our wills so that we will do the will of his Father. He came to write the words of life in our hearts so that in fact we will have God, the Rock, as our solid foundation. It makes all the difference in the world that our Savior Jesus Christ was the speaker of the words in our gospel passage.

This is not to say that we can just forget about the threats of judgment in our gospel reading for today but that we need to hear them in the context of who Jesus was and what he was talking about. He began his teaching that day with all kinds of blessings and promises. "Blessed are the poor in spirit, for theirs is the kingdom of heaven." "Blessed are those who mourn, for they shall be comforted." "Blessed are the meek, for they will inherit the earth." These are not virtues demanded of us; they are gifts given to us; they are promises. They are what we receive as we follow Jesus. His righteousness will fill us; his mercy will make us merciful; his peace will make us peacemakers.

Jesus himself is the primary promise and gift of God and as he comes to us all these other gifts and promises are ours as well. Faith is living in light of the promises. Faith is receiving the gifts. But we often get confused about this. We think that faith means believing the right things, whether that involves theories about the Bible or accepting some ancient creeds or a list of fundamentals or the primacy of the Pope. But that is a hopeless way to think about faith. And that is what Jesus is attacking at the end of the Sermon on the Mount, when he says that it is not sufficient simply to say, "Lord, Lord," because faith involves doing the will of God. When Jesus speaks of those who hear his words and act on them, we get a much better picture of faith.

Faith comes by hearing, the apostle Paul wrote (Romans 10:17), but it is not the same as hearing. It has to do with hearing and doing, as Jesus said. Faith is what happens with us when we hear. In the Bible the word "obedience" is closely related to faith. "Obedience" is not a popular word these days, however. We associate it with taking harsh or meaningless orders in the military or from a boss or a parent. Yet the word "obedience" itself both in its English derivation and in the biblical Greek is related to the word for hearing (look it up in a big dictionary!). Literally, "obedience" means to be "under the hearing," to act on what you have heard. If someone yells "Duck!" and you bend down and a flying object misses you, you have obeyed; you have acted on what you have heard.

This is the picture of faith in the New Testament. That is why Saint Paul can write that faith comes by hearing: It is acting on what we have heard. This is what Jesus is talking about when he says that those who hear his words and do them are truly building their lives on a solid foundation. He is not merely laying out a bunch of conditions for us to meet. Rather, he is emphasizing how important it is for us to hear his words so that they can do something to us, so that they can redirect our lives in accord with God's will.

Yet when we do hear these words, about the wise person who builds his house on the rock, in contrast to the foolish one who builds on sand, it is very tempting to put the emphasis on our building the house instead of on the matter of what the foundation is. In Jesus' illustration, the two foundations (rock and sand) are there and the question is where do we put the house? The focus is not on building the house; presumably both houses were adequate. And the house that stands when the storms rage stands not because its walls are stronger but because it is on the rock, the sure foundation. Likewise, the house that has the great fall when the floods and the winds come falls not because of its own inadequacies but because it is set on grains of sand that are washed away. The point is, everything depends on where persons put their houses, that is, their lives.

Jesus — his words, his deeds, his life, his death and resurrection — is the only sure foundation, the Rock. It is a simple image, but to those first-century hearers it might have said more than we hear at first. All over the Old Testament God is called a rock (compare Deuteronomy 32:4, 31; Psalm 18:2, 31; 28:1; 62:2; Isaiah 17:10). In the days before cement and steel, a rock was one of the strongest things known and so it became a fitting image for God. When Jesus talks about building on a rock, his Israelite hearers would have immediately connected it to God.

Then the zinger in all of this is when Jesus likens hearing *his* words and doing them to building on the rock. This is to equate his words with God! In Jesus' words the true God is coming into our midst. The person who hears Jesus' words is brought by them into God's kingdom. We miss all this if we only think of Jesus as a great teacher or a prophet. Christians believe that he was God in the flesh, God for us. "Don't say anything about God that you cannot say about the man Jesus Christ," remember?

Jesus' words are God's words. We are to hear them, trust them, do them, because we are made by God and these words will shape our lives into what God intends for us. In Jesus we know that God intends love for us, goodness and mercy for us. Because of our sins we may forget this or even not want what God intends for us; we won't see that it is for our good. And so, we need Jesus' words over and over — in speech, in deeds, in song, in poetry, in art — because that is how God comes to us.

[Today we receive Jesus in what the early church called "visible words," the body and blood of Christ which come to us through the bread and wine. Here we can see the elements, hear Christ's words of promise that they are his body and blood for us and know that they bring us forgiveness of sins and new life. Here we can even taste Jesus' words and as we go out from this place we will carry with us the "aftertaste" of his grace for us.] This is the sure foundation on which the wise person will build. How blessed we are to have such a Rock. Amen.

Corpus Christi
John 6:51-58

The Bread Of Life

Nearly the whole sixth chapter of the Gospel of John is about bread. It begins with an account of Jesus feeding a huge crowd of people from five loaves and two fish and doing it so lavishly that there are 12 baskets of crumbs left over. Then, after Jesus and his disciples left by boat, the next day the crowd searched and found him on the other side of the lake, but Jesus criticized them: "You're looking for me for the wrong reasons, just because I gave you lots of food yesterday. But that's really not what you need most; you need the food of eternal life." "But what should we do?" they asked. And Jesus replied, "This is the work of God, that you believe in him whom God has sent."

The crowd was not sure about that and challenged Jesus to do an additional miraculous work of some sort to prove that they should believe in him. They suggested that he should do something to top the Old Testament miracle of manna in the wilderness. But Jesus challenged them by saying that it wasn't Moses who was responsible for giving their ancestors bread from heaven in the first place, it was "my Father" (Jesus said) who is *now* giving the true bread from heaven — not perishable manna but "the one who comes down from heaven and gives life to the world."

Jesus was obviously talking about himself but the crowd was still confused. "Give us some of this bread," they said, somewhat stupidly. Then comes Jesus' first great statement in this chapter (v. 35), "I am the bread of life. Whoever comes to me will never be hungry, and whoever believes in me will never be thirsty." Then he said that God the Father had sent him and he was doing the Father's will.

This extravagant claim aroused Jesus' enemies: "How can he say he's the bread from heaven? This is just Jesus the carpenter. We know his parents. He's not from heaven; he's from Nazareth." And Jesus responded, "You can't understand this because only those whom the Father draws to me can believe. But in fact, no one has seen the Father except me. If you believe in me you will have eternal life, because I am the bread of life. Your ancestors ate manna in the wilderness, but that didn't give them eternal life. I am the living bread that came down from heaven. Whoever eats of this bread will live forever; and the bread I will give for the life of the world is my flesh."

Now we have gotten to the gospel reading for today. Jesus has proclaimed that he is the living bread, the only one who gives eternal life, because he gives his own flesh for the life of the world. For us who know how the story turns out, giving his own flesh is a clear reference to his crucifixion. But the crowd, which seems more and more confused, wonders, "How can this man give us his flesh to eat?"

Then suddenly we hear some new language introduced by Jesus: "Very truly I tell you, unless you eat the flesh of the Son of Man and drink his blood, you have no life in you." First, he speaks of the Son of Man: the one who comes down from heaven at the end of time, according to Old Testament prophecy.When Jesus calls himself the Son of Man he is saying that he is God's long-promised Savior. Then he speaks not only of eating his flesh or eating the bread but also of drinking his blood, which is a clear reference to the Eucharist. Long before the church had articulated any elaborate doctrine of the presence of Christ in the bread and wine, Jesus made it clear that as we eat the bread and drink the wine, we receive his flesh and blood for our salvation. Those who receive this sacrament, he said, "abide in me, and I in them."

Surprisingly, there is no account of the last supper in John's gospel. Yet there is a lot of sacramental language in this writing. By the time John wrote late in the first century, Christians were regularly celebrating the eucharist, so his readers would have heard the story of the institution at the last supper every Sunday. John's concern is not to focus our attention on the sacramental ritual itself but on its essential meaning. What is important is our communion with the crucified and risen Lord Jesus Christ, who meets us now just as he did nearly 2,000 years ago in the breaking of the bread and the pouring of the wine.

Christians have had an unfortunate tendency to understand the eucharist in somewhat mechanical ways. There are exact rules for how it is to be done; detailed theories of how it works; specific rituals to be gone through; and disciplines of preparation, reverence and adoration for us who receive. On top of that, we have sometimes thought of eucharistic grace as a "thing" that we get when we receive the bread — as if we were basically independent, autonomous people who simply need a little help, a little additive, a little grace to set us on our way. So we go through the motions, so to speak, much like the crowd who asked Jesus, "What must we do to perform the works of God?" Jesus' answer to us is the same as to them: "This is the work of God, that you believe in him whom he has sent." It is not that God's grace is quantified so that we can get some, but that we *believe* in Jesus, we trust him in all things, and through faith in him as he himself meets us in the eucharist he abides in us and we in him.

The whole purpose of God sending Jesus, after all, is that the world might believe. The fall of humans into sin takes place when people don't believe God's word, when people don't trust God. To restore people to the way we are meant to be means that we need to be able to trust again. In the incarnation, God became flesh and dwelled among us. The whole life of Jesus Christ — his birth, actions, words, healings, obedience, crucifixion, and resurrection — is *God's* life in the flesh so that we might know him as a God of grace and truth, of mercy and love, and in this we might learn to trust again.

When we celebrate the eucharist, we do so by confessing our sins and professing our faith, by praising the goodness of God, by hearing the biblical stories of how all this came about and remembering and giving thanks for these saving acts on our behalf. More than that, we do so together, as a community — and more than a community, for scripture calls us "the body of Christ." We gather, as the ancient prayer put it, as individual grains of wheat who are going to be joined into one loaf, one body, in Christ.

When we receive the bread, we receive Christ's body. As we receive his body, the bread, we are reconstituted as his body, the church. "The body of Christ" has a multiple meaning as we receive the bread: 1) "*This* is the body of Christ," which is the true bread of heaven which gives eternal life; and 2) "*You* are the body of Christ" and individually members of it. Grace is not something we "get" as individuals and then go our separate ways. Grace is God's *favor* which joins us to him through his Son and joins us to all others who are joined to him.

Do we want all this? Wasn't it simpler to think of the eucharist in private religious ways that didn't make such claims on us? In the next verses in John, chapter 6, it says that the disciples themselves had great difficulty with what Jesus was saying. "This teaching is difficult; who can accept it?" they asked. But Jesus did not comfort them; he challenged them: "Does this offend you? You haven't seen anything yet." And then he speaks both about his being lifted up on the cross and his eventual ascension as being even more offensive.

Does what is promised to us in the eucharist offend us? Threaten us? Wait until you hear the whole story of the crucified one. He will tell us that he is like a grain of wheat which unless it falls into the ground and dies remains a single grain and does not bear fruit (John 12:24). And he adds: Those who love their life lose it; and, whoever serves me must follow me, and where I am, there will my servant be also.

Christ, the bread of life, gives us a kind of life unlike the "good life" of our culture. When we eat the true bread, when we believe in the true God, we begin a new journey, we embark on a new way of life. "Eternal life" is not only life after death; it is a dimension of life already available to us now, through faith in Christ.

So, come to the table with your eyes open wide to the one who is the bread of life, the true bread come down from heaven, who invites you to adore him and receive him, to believe in him and follow him; and who promises to abide in you. Truly, he is the bread of life!

O blest memorial of our dying Lord,
Who living bread to us shall here afford:
Oh, may our souls forever feed on thee,
And thou, O Christ, forever precious be.

— Thomas Aquinas (1227-1274)

Proper 5
Pentecost 3
Ordinary Time 10
Matthew 9:9-13, 18-26 (C)
Matthew 9:9-13 (L, RC)

Friends In Low Places

This gospel reading from Matthew is surprising, if you think about it. A man named Matthew is sitting at his job in the tax collector's booth and Jesus comes to that town and says two words to Matthew, "Follow me." And Matthew stands up, walks off his job and follows Jesus. Does that ring true? Matthew didn't count the cost; he didn't think of the consequences; he just followed. It seems too abrupt and unlikely. Yet this passage is God's word for us today. What shall we make of it?

Part of the difficulty is that we only have this one little bit of a story out of the whole gospel, so it looks like the focus of the story is on Matthew and what happens to him. And perhaps the preacher will tell us to be like Matthew! To which our reaction might well be, "Good grief. I've got a family and a mortgage. I can't just up and leave."

If we all had Bibles in front of us, we would be able to see that some really important things had gone on before Jesus got to Matthew. Jesus had already called the four fishermen, Peter, Andrew, James and John, to be his disciples and he had taught them what discipleship means in the Sermon on the Mount. Not only those four heard Jesus, but huge crowds were listening to him by now and were astonished by what he said and the authority with which he said it.

Between the Sermon on the Mount and our story today there is a series of episodes in which Jesus did amazing things: He healed a leper and the centurion's servant and Peter's mother-in-law; he cast out evil spirits; he even demonstrated power over nature by quieting an awful storm. All this excited the people and many praised him; but it also stirred up opponents from among the religious leaders, who questioned Jesus' authority and feared his popularity. This all came to a head in the event immediately prior to Jesus' call of Matthew (see 9:2-8). Friends brought a paralyzed person to Jesus and Jesus told the person that his sins were forgiven. Jesus' opponents screamed, "That's blasphemy." ("Blasphemy" means putting oneself in the place of God and "no one can forgive sins except God.") Yet since finally everything that threatens human life is rooted in sin, in a broken relationship with God, to heal a person Jesus must also have authority over sin — which he proved by saying to the man, "Rise and walk," and the man did. And it says that when the crowds saw this, they glorified God.

Now we get to Jesus calling Matthew and we see that the story isn't primarily about Matthew; it's about *Jesus.* Jesus is continuing on his journey, announcing the kingdom of God and calling people to follow him, when he comes up to Matthew. Probably Matthew had already heard of Jesus, since the crowds had spread the word, but it is clear that the focus of our passage is not on how Matthew made his decision or on what sort of a person he was. The focus is on the Son of God confronting Matthew and, rather than denouncing him for working for the occupying government and betraying his people or even inquiring into his qualifications, Jesus simply tells him to follow. No sales pitch, no promises, no deals; just "Follow me." This was the same way Jesus had called Peter and the others. He found disciples who didn't even know they were lost until long after they'd been found.

"Follow me" was a word that had unlocked Peter and the others from their previous lives. Now it liberated Matthew from his collaboration. It was a powerful word that could tear persons away from things they had made too important, from commitments and habits and situations that made them less than God wanted them to be.

Then what happened? It seems that in finding Matthew Jesus also found Matthew's friends and associates and so he and his disciples stayed and ate with them. Matthew's friends, not surprisingly, were the same sort that he was, which gave the righteous religious leaders an easy target in going after Jesus. We can hear their shocked voices as they asked the disciples, "Why does your teacher eat with tax collectors and sinners?" (They were implying that Jesus could not be sent from God if he behaved this way, since scripture has all sorts of prohibitions against associating with sinners.) But that is not only the Pharisees' question; it is the question of good people of every age. And so, when Jesus heard their question, he replied with God's true word — for them and possibly also for us.

"Those who are well have no need of a doctor, but those who are sick." At one level this is simply common sense. Jesus is saying that he came to minister to those in need. Yes, but, we think, "That's very dangerous. It opens the door to all sorts of arguments about who Jesus came for." Jesus knew that at the level of common sense, his statement could be debated. So he turned to scripture: "Go and learn what this means," he said, and the quoted a Bible verse (from Hosea 6:6), where God says, "I desire mercy, not sacrifice." Sacrifice in the Bible is what's offered to God — prayer, fasting, burnt offerings, doing the proper rituals, keeping separate from sinful people and situations. Mercy is love offered to other people. Despite many of the Old Testament laws about avoiding impurity, Jesus here claims that it is more important to God that we do works of love for others than that we offer sacrifice to him.

Not only is this God's will for us, but it is the way God *is* with us, as that is revealed here in Jesus' words: "I have come to call not the righteous but sinners." "That's what I did with Matthew,'' Jesus is saying. ''That's what I did with the leper, with the centurion's servant and with the people possessed with demons.'' Someone has translated Jesus' words as ''I did not come to invite good people; I came for bad people.'' That puts it sharply and causes us to wonder whether it means that good people should become bad (which can't be right) or to realize that perhaps we aren't so good (which may be closer to the truth).

The Bible says, ''There is no one who is righteous, not even one'' (Romans 3:10). If Jesus did not call sinners, there would be no one to call. To be a disciple is not to be one who has all the right qualifications but to be one who has been set free from sin. Matthew was liberated from being a collaborator by the call to follow. It all happened at Jesus' initiative. It is all by God's grace alone. As Jesus said in another place, ''You did not choose me; I chose you'' (John 15:6).

Several years ago the country-western singer Garth Brooks had a hit song titled ''I've Got Friends In Low Places.'' It's the story of a young man whose girlfriend has dumped him to marry an older and wealthier man. The young man shows up at her wedding, but he doesn't have the right clothes or behavior and so he stomps off in anger to join his hard-living friends, telling her, ''I've got friends in low places, where the whiskey flows and the beer chases the blues away . . . .'' Raucous words, but set to a powerful melody. I've often thought as I've listened to the song on the radio that with a slight change these words could apply to God-in-Christ: ''*He's* got friends in low places.'' Perhaps even, ''He's got friends in low places, where the mercy flows and the free grace is for you and me . . . .''

''Friends in Low Places.'' It's the picture of God we see in Jesus' call of Matthew and his eating with Matthew's friends. More than that, it is good news for us. The Great Physician comes for those who are sick. The merciful one comes for those who are in need. The Son of God comes to call sinners. To us, as to all the people in the gospels, he says, ''Follow me.'' He doesn't ask for credentials; he doesn't make bargains; he doesn't offer a deal; he simply calls people to himself. "Follow me." He's got friends in low places. That's why we can be sure that we're welcome. As it is written, "I have come to call not the righteous but sinners." That's why the call to discipleship includes us.

[Today, as if to drive home the point, just as on the day that Jesus called Matthew and ate with him and his friends, the risen Christ who calls us would eat and drink with us, in the meal of bread and wine. He stoops to be in the company of sinners and offers himself as our nourishment, giving us through his body and blood in this meal the forgiveness of all our sins, new life, and salvation. Thank God, he's got friends in low places.]

There is one last piece for us to think about today, even as we worship the Lord who accepts us just as we are. Some people have tended to turn this gospel message (of Jesus accepting us just the way we are) into an excuse to remain sinful. They have gotten it right that Jesus came to call sinners altogether apart from any merit or worthiness on our part, but they have gone on to draw the conclusion that this means that it is okay to be sinners. That's not the way it happened in our gospel passage and that's not the way God works now either.

Jesus came to Matthew the collaborator with the occupying government; Jesus ate with Matthew and his tax collector friends. Clearly, Jesus reached out to sinners; he had friends in low places. But he said to them, "Follow me. Come after me. Be my disciple." Jesus accepted them just the way they were, *and* (not "but") . . . *and he loved them too much to leave them that way*! His call to follow gave them a new master, a new direction, a new freedom, and a new understanding of what was good and right and true.

Indeed, it is not surprising that only Matthew, of all the gospel writers, includes the account of the last judgment (Matthew 25:31-46) in which so much emphasis is put on the importance of people doing acts of kindness for the hungry and the naked and the sick and the prisoners. Matthew's life was transformed by Jesus from one focused on gaining wealth by collecting taxes from others to one of service to those in need.

So also with us: Jesus accepts us just the way we are. Proud or broken, angry or sorrowful, arrogant or hopeless, committers of sins or omitters of good — Jesus accepts us without demanding that we first be worthy. *And* he loves us too much to leave us in our sin. That's the promise in his words, "Follow Me." [And now, our Lord would eat and drink with us. He stoops to be in this company of sinners and offers himself as our nourishment — counting us as his friends in this place.] Thanks be to God. Amen.

Proper 6
Pentecost 4
Ordinary Time 11
Matthew 9:35—10:8 (C, L)
Matthew 9:36—10:8 (RC)

Details

It's probably not a good idea to speed-read the Bible. You might get the overall story and you might even improve your comprehension but you would be likely to miss the little details. And in our passage today from Matthew 9-10 the details are at least as important as the story of the events themselves — and the details may be more interesting.

The story has to do with Jesus seeing all the people in need of God's blessings and commissioning the twelve disciples to do something about it. All the disciples are named and then Jesus gives them some initial instructions for their mission. In our impatience we may want to keep reading quickly through chapter 10 to see what happens. But nothing much happens! Instead, the focus is on Jesus' lengthy instructions and we never do hear what happened to the twelve disciples. Worse than that, it is difficult to see what sort of a word of God this is for *us*.

We need to slow down and look at the details. "When Jesus saw the crowds, he had *compassion* for them" (9:36). We know that word: "compassion." It's used a lot these days. But in the New Testament it is almost always used of God (and of Jesus). There is only one time it is used of another human being and that one — appropriately enough — is the good

Samaritan. That should tell us that here we have to do with an important detail. The whole reason for the mission on which the disciples are sent is the compassion of the Son of God. If we are mission-minded, we might learn something from this. Mission does not begin with God's anger that some persons are sinners; mission does not begin with humanly-constructed goals for institutional growth; mission does not come primarily from our obedience to God's commandments to go and make disciples. Mission all starts in the compassionate heart of God.

"Compassion" in the biblical languages literally means "to feel in the viscera": to feel in your guts or in your heart. Here Jesus sees the people of Israel harassed and helpless and he feels for them, he *hurts* for them. And the details keep coming. The people were "harassed and helpless," it says; literally, "mangled and miserable," almost "limping and desperate." Why? Because they were "like sheep without a shepherd." Not just needy in general — depressed, sick or discouraged — but needy because they didn't have a good shepherd, a good ruler, a good master. It is a larger sort of need than we ordinarily tend to think of.

Maybe the best image here is that the people are oppressed — perhaps by bad religion, bad philosophy or bad politics. "Shepherd," after all, is a common biblical image for the political and religious leaders of Israel. Jesus here is speaking of the most profound sort of need that people have — which shows itself in so many of our more obvious needs. The cure for such a profound need is not a pay raise or a new health care plan or therapy or a vacation, as important as all these things are. The cure is to have the right God, the true shepherd. All that from one verse: Don't miss the details.

What happens when the compassion of God is confronted by a huge need? We know all about huge needs: massive starvation, horrible wars, homelessness, high rates of divorce and out-of-wedlock births, diseases that seem out of control. We usually speak of these as tragic or catastrophic. But Jesus looks at the need of the people and sees it as an opportunity: "The harvest is plentiful'' (9:37). He likens the great need to a great crop that needs to be harvested.

Exactly this same sort of thing goes on today in our conversations about mission. Some moan about our society's increasing secularism. Others get very worried about cities and states with very low percentages of Christians. But for some Christians this means an opportunity. There are people who need to hear the gospel! The harvest is plentiful.

What's needed? Laborers. Workers. More workers are needed to bring in the crop. Well, let's get out the time and talent sheets. Who will volunteer? Whoa! Watch the details. Jesus did not ask for volunteers from among the disciples or anyone else. What did he say? ''The laborers are few; therefore ask the Lord . . .'' (9:38). The need is great, so pray to *God* to do something about it. So un-American; so impractical. But the point is that we do not make ourselves into missionaries or any other co-worker of God. We are to ask God to do it. It is not our mission after all; it is God's.

The old question asks why conservative churches grow. There are lots of cynical or merely pragmatic answers to that question, but the biblical answer might be that they *pray*. Where there is little prayer, there is little mission. Prayer is what gets our wills aligned with God's will. That is absolutely necessary if God is going to give us authority over anything.

One more detail in these two verses. Jesus speaks of laborers, workers. ''Worker'' is a very unpretentious word. Jesus doesn't say we should pray that God will send heroes or all-stars or experts or innovators, but workers. These workers are not to sow but to reap; they don't have to invent but complete. Basically, workers need to be willing and able to do what needs to be done. That is what Jesus says to pray for: workers that God will send out, literally, push out, to make disciples.

Then, as if in answer to prayer, Jesus (God's Word!) provided laborers by summoning his twelve disciples (10:1). They aren't called ''rulers'' or ''princes of the church'' but ''disciples,'' followers, servants (see Matthew 20:25-28). And he didn't call them because of their superb qualifications but instead it says that he *gave* them divine gifts: authority to cast out evil spirits and to heal. What this means, in effect, is that Jesus gave them gifts to do what he was doing — ministering to people's total well-being.

Next comes a very interesting detail, so small that we might easily read right past it. "These are the names of the twelve apostles:" (and then they are all listed). Did you notice? Everywhere else in Matthew the twelve are called "disciples," but here, just this once, they are called "apostles." That means the "sent ones." Like letters, you can hear the word "post" in apostles. The twelve here are called by a functional term connoting not status but mission. That's something to remember when we think about the church as being apostolic: not that it is ruled by successors to the apostles but that we today like those twelve are part of Christ's ongoing mission.

Then look at that list (10:2-4). They are all named and we remember that several were fishermen, probably not highly educated. One is so little known that it is added that he is the son of Alphaeus. The point for us is that Christ's mission is carried out by sinners transformed by grace, not by saints without any problems. Only one name includes his former occupation: Matthew the gospel writer calls himself the "tax collector," as if to underline God's amazing grace. Small details, but reassuring to those of us who don't think that God could have any use for persons like us.

Our passage finishes with just the beginnings of Jesus' instructions to his disciples before they go out. But what strange instructions. He says that they should not go to the Gentiles or to the Samaritans, but only to the lost sheep of Israel. Yet we know from other parts of the New Testament that the Christian mission went explicitly to the Gentiles and in the Great Commission it is clearly directed to all nations (Matthew 28:19). What's going on? Here is a seemingly little detail that might have large and even negative implications (for example, in support of Christian anti-Semitism).

These verses (10:5-6) begin by noting that Jesus gives these instructions to "these twelve" disciples and not to all disciples in all times and places. The twelve's target in this mission is the lost sheep of Israel. Israel was given first chance. Jesus came for them first. By the time this gospel was written, perhaps 40 to 50 years after Jesus' death, the Gentile mission was the main thing. Including the account of this first sending of the twelve reminds us that the mission to the Gentiles will never cancel but will always include the mission to the lost sheep of Israel. A detail here that just cannot be seen in English is found in the force of the Greek form of the word "go"; it has the effect of saying *keep going* to the lost sheep of Israel. It would seem to press in the direction of a continuing mission to Israel, even though this is not popular among many Christians today.

This issue cannot be solved with one little verse. But it can be clarified by the final two verses of our passage (10:7-8), in which Jesus begins to tell the twelve what they are to say and do. "Proclaim the good news," which is, "The kingdom of heaven has come near." The disciples are to realize that God's kingdom comes right in their words. It's not a message here of repentance and coming doom but one of joy and excitement. It's good news! Jesus is for you. Now.

Then the deeds: again, the verb forms speak of continuing actions: "By curing the sick, raising the dead, cleansing lepers, casting out demons." These things are what Jesus has been doing up till now. He calls his disciples to continue in his work. Jesus is present in his disciples; they are his body. Through them he continues to act. He will act; the only question is whether he will also act through us. Pray the Lord to send out laborers. Only a verb form; just a mere detail. Yet the sense that each of the verbs is ongoing makes the back-and-forth relationship between the first century and ours very apparent. We are not the twelve; our mission is not only to Israel. Yet Jesus' words to them also have importance for us as we look at them today.

By encouraging us to look closely at the details of this passage, what have I been doing? Is it only an exercise in Bible study? Is it just a short course on how to read a text closely? I hope not.

The great German-American architect of this century, Ludwig Mies van der Rohe, is known for his exhaustively planned buildings. In his skyscrapers every aspect of the interior and exterior is coordinated into a single ideal. Nothing essential is omitted; nothing that is included is out of place. The statement is attributed to Mies van der Rohe that "God is in the details." The perfection of the whole depends on the perfection of the details. The meaning of the whole is inseparable from each of the smallest details. God is in the details.

I suggest that his statement may also apply to reading the Bible. Concentrating on the details is not mere scholarly pedantry or fundamentalist superstition; rather, it is a way of seeing the Word in the words. Slowing down for the details forces us to attend to the passage so that it can become God's word for us. The compassion of Christ; the plentiful harvest but the need to pray for laborers; Jesus' gifts for mission; his calling ordinary people to be disciples; the emphasis on the continuing mission of Christ. God's word is in the details. Indeed, may we not say that God is in the details? Think about it. Amen.

Proper 7
Pentecost 5
Ordinary Time 12
Matthew 10:24-29 (C)
Matthew 10:24-33 (L)
Matthew 10:26-33 (RC)

Stop Being Afraid

Jesus' instructions to his disciples prior to their first mission continue in today's gospel reading. He has been telling them about all the dangers and hardships they may have to put up with and ends by saying (in effect), "What do you expect? A disciple is not greater than his teacher. If the world gives me a bad time, it will give you one too" (Matthew 10:24-25).

So what does Jesus do? Sell them life insurance? Give them bullet-proof vests? Teach them how to diffuse conflict? Hardly. Instead he says, "Don't ever be afraid of your enemies and critics. Even though it's not obvious now, the truth will come out finally. So, speak up; shout it out; stand and deliver" (10:26-27). Oh, my. We don't want to be heroes, especially not religious ones. It's all we can do to get to church on Sundays and we're supposed to be shouting the word of God from the housetops? No way. We're afraid.

But Jesus doesn't quit. "Stop being afraid" (that's the force of the verb); "stop being afraid" — not just once but always. "Stop being afraid of people who can kill the body but not the soul." The point is, people can hurt us only temporarily because life comes from God. Even if they kill us, God the author of life will raise us. "Don't fear people; fear God" (the one who can kill both body and soul) (10:28).

Contrary to popular opinion, Jesus is saying that the voice of the people is *not* the voice of God. We worry way too much about what other people say or think of us and far too little about what God thinks of us. Yes, but .... We know this is true. We've heard it before. But, it's easier said than done.

So what's the solution? More advice? More instruction? That's what we would expect. But Jesus is not only a teacher. He is the revelation of God, though he doesn't stop being a good teacher when he opens a window into God. He says, "Aren't sparrows the most common and cheapest bird around? Yet not one of them dies apart from God your Father" (10:29). Wow. "And what about you?" Jesus asks. "God even knows every hair on your head. So stop being afraid. You are of much more value than any sparrow" (10:30-31).

Isn't that amazing? God knows everything that we go through and nothing that happens to us escapes him. Even if we die, it doesn't happen apart from God. Even if we seem totally abandoned, even if our prayers don't seem to be answered, even if everything seems hopeless, God knows and God cares. If that's the case, we can stop being afraid.

Not being afraid isn't something that *we* can accomplish. As long as we think it is, we will still be afraid — of other people, of death, of circumstances (real or imagined). But as Jesus reveals it, we can stop being afraid because of a *promise* — a promise that God who watches over even the commonest of birds will take care of us.

When someone makes a promise to you, what do you have to do? If your grandparents write their will and say that when they die you will get the farm, what do you have to do? Be nice to them? Work really hard? Why? They have already promised you the farm. "What do I have to do?" is the wrong response to a promise. It doesn't make sense. If you find out you are going to inherit something, you say "Hooray! Wonderful! Thank you." Out of the blue you have a retirement plan. Suddenly the future doesn't seem so uncertain.

Most of our life is lived not according to "the logic of promise" but in asking and answering the question "What do I have to do?" If I want to graduate from school, what must I do? If I want to get promoted, what must I do? If I want to be respected, what should I do? Nothing wrong with that. Those are all important things that we can work on. Most of life is like that.

What goes wrong is when we try to put that "logic" of "What do I have to do?" into our religious life. "What do I have to do to get God to care about me?" Stop being afraid? No, no, no. It's the other way around. God does care about you so you don't have to be afraid. The response to a demand — to graduate from school, to support your family, to be someone others respect — is to do something. The response to a promise is altogether different. The response to a promise is to celebrate, rejoice, give thanks — because someone else has done something. God knows every hair on your head. God even cares about sparrows and you are of much more value than any sparrow. God will take care of you. That's a promise. You don't have to be afraid. Ever.

Yes, but .... Who can believe this? Who can live without fear? We are suspicious even of promises. We are always hearing promises that aren't kept. Our grandparents may promise to leave us the farm when they die, but who's to say they won't go bankrupt and lose the farm long before that? Husbands and wives promise to be faithful to each other until death, but half the time they can't keep those promises. Our life experience teaches us to be suspicious of promises, not because people who make promises don't have good intentions but because fallible, mortal, sinful human beings like us can't always keep our promises. "I promise that I'll repay you that money ... if I possibly can." "I'll be there promptly at noon ... if I don't have a car accident." "I will finish remodeling the house ... if I don't die first."

All of our promises have an "if" in them — "if I can"; "if I don't have an accident"; "if I don't die." We can't help it. It has nothing to do with bad intentions. It is the way we are. We cannot make promises without conditions, without "ifs."

Yet Jesus made many incredibly far-reaching promises. Not only about God knowing every hair on our heads and promising to care for us, but also remember some of the others: "Today, you will be with me in paradise." "I go to prepare a place for you." "Lo, I am with you always." "I tell you, your sins are forgiven." And the Beatitudes (Matthew 5:3-12): those who mourn will be comforted, the meek will inherit the earth, the pure in heart will see God, and so forth. But when Jesus was crucified, these promises seemed to be all cancelled out. He had failed. He was just a dreamer, one more idealistic prophet making promises he couldn't keep. Even his disciples no longer followed. In the accounts in Matthew, Mark, and Luke they are nowhere to be seen at the crucifixion. "All of them deserted him and fled" (Mark 14:50). And Peter denied even knowing Jesus.

You can't live on promises alone, this would seem to say. Yet the gospel of salvation is nothing but promises. The gospel is always a word about what will be the case forever, a word that opens the future to us, that frees us from being afraid. Is the gospel only a dream, then? Is it just an illusion? Merely a possibly helpful fiction? Something to help us die more serenely?

It would be if Jesus' death were the end of the story. For us death is the end of the story; we cannot make unconditional promises because the threat of death means that we can never be sure of keeping our promises. But God raised Jesus. God made sure that Jesus could keep his promises. Even death (our death) will not keep Jesus from keeping the promises he makes to us in the Bible, because we die with him and we will be raised with him. That's a promise. And it's the basis for our hope in all the other promises. Even the sparrows don't fall to the ground apart from God the Father and we are of greater value than many sparrows.

Therefore, it is the case, as Jesus says, that "Everyone who acknowledges me before others, I also will acknowledge before my Father in heaven'' (Matthew 10:32). That's a promise. But we can even mess that up if we look at it through our ''old'' eyes of experience rather than seeing it in light of the death and resurrection of the one who said these words.

We can wrongly understand these words to be telling us that *if* we acknowledge or confess Christ, *then* he will bless us by acknowledging us to God. But Jesus is talking to his disciples, who already have been confessing their faith in him; he is saying to them and to all who follow him that they will never be let down because he himself will acknowledge them before God. That's a promise.

One commentator translates this verse: ''Every person who *stands up for me* in front of others, I will *stand up for* that person in front of my Father in heaven.'' It is that sort of rock-solid guarantee, a promise won through the fires of crucifixion, that enables us to stop being afraid of people and circumstances and shout the gospel from the housetops. Fear of God as we know God through Christ bestows fearlessness of people and circumstances that might otherwise cause us to lose faith.

The final verse is a somber spelling out of the reverse. If we deny Jesus, if we say, with Peter, ''I do not know the man'' (Matthew 26:72), and even swear to drive home the point, then Jesus will also say he doesn't know us. No one will be forced into the kingdom. Even that is a promise, although it must be understood in light of Peter's bitter weeping when he realizes what he has done and the subsequent word of the angel at the tomb to be sure to include Peter in the news that Jesus is risen (Mark 16:7) and the marvelous account of Jesus' threefold restoration of Peter (John 21:15-19) after the resurrection.

Today that same crucified and risen Lord is in our midst, allowing us to stop being afraid because of the powerful love of God on which the promise is based: ''Even the hairs of your head are all counted; you are of more value than many sparrows.'' [The promise continues in the blessed sacrament as we hear Jesus say that ''this bread is my body, given for you,'' and "this wine is my blood, shed for you." We receive Christ in the bread and wine because he promises to meet us there. In this sacrament the promise is visible and touchable and feelable and tastable. "Take and eat; take and drink." As we do this in remembrance of him, we can stop being afraid.] Amen.

Proper 8
Pentecost 6
Ordinary Time 13
Matthew 10:40-42 (C)
Matthew 10:34-42 (L)
Matthew 10:37-42 (RC)

Welcoming Christ

What is this passage about? Is it about the disciples, the twelve? Yes, of course, it is about them; these are Jesus' final words of instruction to them and astonishing words they are! "Whoever welcomes you guys welcomes me," Jesus says, "and whoever welcomes me welcomes the Father who sent me" (10:40). Their mission was God's mission; their words were God's words; the people whom they met encountered God in them and their teachings.

These are strong words, but we know that these disciples (minus Judas) turned the whole world upside down with their proclamation. Whoever welcomed them did indeed welcome Christ and the one who sent him.

But what is this passage about for today? These disciples are long gone. Do the words still apply? How do we welcome them and in so doing welcome Christ and the Father? One way is by receiving their witness, by joyfully believing the New Testament gospel. When we receive the message that they wrote down for us, we receive Christ. It's the old, old story, as the hymn says, but it's new in every generation and those who want to hear it the most are those who already know it best. Faith comes by hearing, as the apostle Paul wrote, hearing the word of Christ (Romans 10:17) as it was spoken and written by the disciples and by others who were converted by their words.

This is why we call the church "apostolic": it lives on in the teachings handed down by the apostles, those ones who were sent on a mission, through whom Christ himself came to people. The church is not a club of like-minded individuals; it is not a voluntary organization gathered to do good or meet needs (important as these things may be); it is not a powerful institution whose product is religion. The church is a body of believers who welcome the apostles' teaching — who trust it and live it and continue the mission.

Nobody begins to be a Christian all by himself or herself though. At the very least, someone would have to help us learn to read before we could accept the message of the Bible. But in most cases we don't learn the gospel first by reading it but by hearing it — from our parents and relatives, Sunday school teachers and pastors. Christians have sometimes distinguished between the written word and the "living word," reserving that last phrase for the spoken or proclaimed word in which the gospel comes alive for us through the words of another spoken directly to us. The apostolic witness, in other words, comes to us through present day "apostles" and witnesses.

This brings it awfully close to home, however. This would seem to suggest that as we welcome Christian workers today, as we welcome other Christians bearing witness to their faith, we receive Christ. Yes! And also, those who welcome us, who receive us, receive Christ. That's quite a claim! But it shouldn't surprise us, if we think about it. The Christian faith spread for centuries without a written New Testament. The sixteenth century reformer Martin Luther once said that it was a shame that God's Word had to be written down because it was meant to be spoken, to encounter us in a way that our reading the words may not always do as effectively.

These verses are not only speaking of the gospel message or the spoken or written word, however, but also of the speakers, the Christian persons who bring the message. That becomes clear in verses 40-41 where very specific people and actions are mentioned. It has to do with what many biblical scholars today are calling "Hospitality": the friendly, warm, respectful receiving of people in the name of Christ. Such hospitality transcends our usual application of it to family and friends (see vv. 36-39!), because it has to do specifically with receiving prophets or righteous persons "in the name of" a prophet or a righteous person.

The Bible here is not speaking of some sort of generic hospitality but of the sort that we give to certain people because we believe they speak for God or are before us as believers in Christ. This could mean financial support for ministers and missionaries or for fellow believers who are down on their luck. Or, to turn it around, if we are those who come as Christians we are to be aware that people relate to us in light of our faith and witness. That is really obvious to one who is a religious professional. If we get a speeding ticket or are heard using profanity or do not speak out against wrongdoing, people criticize us (and rightly so). But that ought to be the case for all Christians: our behavior ought to reflect our belief; our conduct ought to square with our confession.

It goes much deeper than this, however. It is not only our character or sincerity that are at stake. If we relate to others as disciples and if people relate to us as believers, we and they are really seeking to relate not only to those persons but also to *Jesus* and to the one who sent him. Someone has written that when church members call on people who have stopped attending worship and other congregational activities we should never accept at face value the reasons such people offer for staying away. These reasons often have to do with being offended by someone or by some change in the congregation. Such reasons may be real enough and should not be ignored, but they are symptoms. The actual reason (this writer claims) is a crisis of *faith* — which means that if they are to be reached it will be through their encountering Christ who is the source and goal of faith through us and through other Christians.

Ministers often learn this the hard way. People come to us with psychological or economic or health problems and we give in to the temptation to try to solve those problems as counselors or by giving money or advice, when the reason that the people came to us in the first place was because they needed to pray or confess their sins or simply receive encouragement from one through whom they could receive Christ. They are "welcoming" us into their struggles in the sense of verse 40 and we blow it by not speaking and living the apostolic word.

Simply the fact that people know you are a believer is a way for those outside the church to make some kind of contact with God. It may be very indirect; it may take many years; you, the believer, may never even know that anything has occurred. But in our passage Jesus praises even the simplest act of giving a cup of water to someone. Getting up on Sunday morning and going to worship may be an eloquent witness in some neighborhoods. Getting involved in the community's issues and tasks and standing up for certain values and principles may also communicate who your Lord is. Discipleship and evangelism are much wider than we usually think . . . if Christ is in us and meets people who meet us.

"Welcoming Christ" refers first of all to welcoming his original disciples and receiving Christ through their word. Second, it refers to the way in which Christ is communicated through believers' words and lives today; in this sense, we Christians are both givers and receivers of Christ, which is an awesome and joyful thing. But there is a third sense in which we need to speak of welcoming Christ, which might be called the "churchly" sense. We finally receive the apostles' witness and Christ and the Father who sent him by being part of Christ's church. Here is where the gospel is treasured and handed on through preaching and teaching, baptizing and receiving the Lord's supper, consoling and encouraging, helping and evangelizing.

To welcome Christ finally means to welcome Christian people by joining with them in being the church and in that way receiving Christ and the Father. Very specific. Very concrete.

Very offensive, in many cases. But experience teaches that people who reject the community of Christian believers and stay away from worship almost inevitably lose their connection with Christ as well. With no word, no sacraments, no prayers, no fellowship, there is no contact with disciples through whom Christ can be welcomed.

This should be taken as a warning by each of us about our own involvement in Christ's church so that we may continue to welcome him. But it should also be a warning to us as a Christian congregation about shaping our life together — our worship, our witness, our budget, our mission, our lifestyles — in such a way that people are able to meet Christ in us and will not meet either no one at all or some other god.

If we reflect on how we have come to be believers, much of this will be obvious. Christ has come to us through the biblical gospel conveyed by people and it has been nourished in us through the larger Christian community. We now need to continue that apostolic task as well as continuing to welcome Christ into our own lives each day. But there is one more twist that we should see in these verses.

Not only do we receive *Christ* through his followers but when we receive Christ we receive the one who sent him. In him, we meet *God*. That's the central Christian confession. That's why the apostle preaches "Jesus Christ, and him crucified" (1 Corinthians 2:2). Christ is the one in whom the true God comes to us. [When today we receive our Lord's body and blood under the signs of bread and wine, God himself enters into us in all his fullness. The forgiveness of sins we receive in this sacrament is divine forgiveness. The host of this meal is the living God, the Creator renewing the creation. The Lord's supper is not a memorial meal for a dead hero but communion with our risen, living Lord and Savior. Just as we receive Christ and him who sent him as we receive one of his disciples, in this meal we receive Christ and the Father through this bread and wine, these means of grace.] "Whoever welcomes me, welcomes the one who sent me." Amen. Come, Lord Jesus!

Proper 9
Pentecost 7
Ordinary Time 14
Matthew 11:16-19, 25-30 (C)
Matthew 11:25-30 (L, RC)

The Promising Invitation[1]

Our gospel reading today contains one of the most familiar passages in the Bible. Most of us probably know it in words of one of the older translations, but most of us *do* know it. "Come unto me, all ye that labor and are heavy laden, and I will give you rest" (Matthew 11:28, KJV). For centuries this passage has been used for comforting the grieving, encouraging the struggling, and giving hope when all else seems to have failed. We read it; we underline it; we memorize it. We trust these words when nothing else seems trustworthy.

"Come unto me." It is a wonderful invitation from our Lord himself. "Come to me, all you that are weary and are carrying heavy burdens, and I will give you rest. Take my yoke upon you, and learn from me; for I am gentle and humble in heart, and you will find rest for your souls. For my yoke is easy, and my burden is light" (11:28-30). It's not only an invitation; it's also a promise: "You will find rest for your souls; my yoke is easy." The words themselves can ease our situation and enliven hope.

It is strange, then, that though we know these words so well, if you're like me you probably have little sense of their original setting in Matthew's gospel. The danger in this is that if we do not know their setting, we may misappropriate them and take them to mean things that Jesus could not have meant or — worse — we may not see where they really do apply most profoundly.

Clearly, Jesus couldn't have meant that in this life all our weariness and burdens of work, poor health, poverty, and the like will disappear. The life of the Christian is not just staying in bed! One day all our burdens will be lifted, but here Jesus is not speaking primarily of eternal life in heaven. He is speaking to his followers in the midst of their participation in his mission. "Come to me now and I will give you rest now. Take my yoke upon you." What is this rest? What is this "yoke" of Christ's that we are to take upon us, a yoke that is easy?

Here is where we need to see the setting in which these familiar words were spoken. Jesus himself is discouraged and even angry, as we see from the earlier parts of chapter 11. Even John the Baptist seems not to have understood what was happening. Then Jesus unloads against "the cities in which most of his deeds of power have been done, because they did not repent" (11:20). The Israelite cities were refusing his deeds and his message, while if such deeds had been done in pagan cities (even in Sodom!) they would have repented, Jesus says.

In his disappointment and rage, what does Jesus do? Here's where our gospel passage starts. It's a prayer. Okay, that's not so hard to understand. But it's a prayer of *thanks*, of all things. "I thank you, Father, Lord of heaven and earth, because you have hidden these things from the wise and intelligent and revealed them to infants" (11:25). Jesus may be disappointed and angry but he is not discouraged by an unresponsive world because he trusts in the Father's sovereignty over all creation. "Thank you, Father; you've hidden the gospel from the wise and well-educated and revealed it only to the little ones," Jesus says, "for such was your gracious will" (11:26).

What's Jesus talking about? What are "these things" that are hidden from the wise and the "such" that is God's will? He is talking about God's radical focusing of the divine word and work in the person and ministry of this one man, Jesus Christ. That's what the wise and the learned back then and in every age have such difficulty seeing. And let's not exclude ourselves. Aren't we also offended or at least puzzled by what Jesus goes on to say next? "All things [absolutely everything] have been handed over to me by my Father; and no one [really] knows the Son except the Father, and no one [really] knows the Father except the Son and anyone to whom the Son chooses to reveal him" (11:27).

The point is not just the obvious one that God's ways are not our ways and that God in some sense is always unknown to mere humans. Of course, there is some truth in that, but it's not the truth of which Jesus is speaking here. Jesus is saying that God the Father has given everything over to the Son; *there is no God apart from the Son.* None of us really fathoms that on our own; only God the Father really knows the Son. But more than that, despite all the knowledge of God claimed by people of all ages and religions, no one really knows the Father except Jesus, the Son, and those to whom the Son reveals him. Such is the Father's gracious will.

It is at this point, with the whole reality and power and being of God concentrated in Jesus that he speaks the familiar words, "Come to *me* . . . and I will give you rest." He is not talking about a vacation; he is not referring to some eternal rest far in the future. He is speaking of our being *connected* to God. Saint Augustine said that our hearts are restless until they find their rest in God. We find our rest in God when we come to Jesus. We find everything there is to know of God in Jesus.

Not in Christianity. Not in the church. Not in some denomination. Not in the Bible, even. Not in doctrines or beliefs. Not in the ten commandments. In Jesus. "Come to *me*," he says. Of course, it is likely that we have found Jesus through Christianity, through the church, in the Bible. But insofar as all of these things — Christianity, church, denomination, Bible, doctrines, commandments — have been created and articulated with the help of human individuals and communities, they themselves are not God. Even the commandments themselves were given because of sin.

All of these things may be instruments that God can use to reach us but they may also be obstacles — things that get between us and God. It is not without reason that people say they cannot believe in God because of Christianity. Horrible things have been done by Christians and in the name of Christianity that certainly aren't conducive to belief in God. The same is true of the church: many have found the church and its teachings, structures, practices and traditions to be anything but godly; people spend years getting over the psychological damage they have suffered from some church. Likewise, the Bible and the commandments can be used like clubs to beat us down and make us feel worthless or they can be interpreted in such irrational and superstitious ways that thinking persons simply throw up their hands in despair.

This is nothing new. Religion and moral laws have always verged on being oppressive, most likely because they come with so much "weight" attached to them because we believe they have to do with God. It was no different in Jesus' time. When he spoke of being weary from carrying heavy burdens it is likely that he was thinking specifically of the burden of religion with its laws and demands. Really? Can that be true?

The clue to this interpretation is in Jesus' use of the word "yoke." A "yoke" is a wooden frame that holds two oxen or other animals side-by-side to enable them to work together to pull a wagon or a plow. It is a burden under which they grow weary. A yoke-shaped device was also an ancient symbol of defeat and slavery, when conquered people were made to wear such a thing. In other words, a yoke was both an actual burden and a symbol of oppression and is often used in a symbolic way in the Bible.

Both the Bible itself and rabbinic teaching speak of the law as a "yoke." (See Acts 15:10 for an example of using yoke negatively. The Rabbis meant this in a positive way in terms of glorious obedience to God that freed people from the obligations of the world.) Jesus contrasts our coming to him and "putting on Christ" (Romans 13:14) with the burdensome yoke of all kinds of law, whether expressed in commandments or in religious dogmas or in Christian institutions. "Learn from me," he says. Not, "do this or else," but "Take my yoke upon you, and learn from me .... My yoke is easy [gentle, kind]. Learn from me."

He does not mean that Christianity is a lark. He still uses the word "yoke," after all, but we might think of it as a new way of carrying life, a new way of bearing responsibilities. As we *learn* from him, as we take his words seriously, which is what taking his yoke upon us means, we will find a new kind of peace and balance that will not be burdensome but freeing and refreshing. (And if we are not finding that peace in our church, maybe we are not hearing the gospel, the "good news," the preaching of the Christ who lived and died for us, through whom we are made right with God altogether apart from our own accomplishments. It is terribly important for Christians to distinguish the gospel from the law and not turn Jesus into a new lawgiver.) His yoke is easy in the sense that it becomes not only our duty but our delight.

To take Christ's yoke upon us (his words, his teachings) is to learn from *him*. His yoke is not a system, not a law, not a religion but communion with a risen, living person through his word and sacraments. As if to underscore this personal aspect, Jesus adds, "For I am gentle and humble in heart" (11:29): "God with a human face," as someone has said. In Christ, God stoops to us and becomes available and approachable. The righteous person (scripture says) lives by faith, by trust. Faith, trust, is a personal relationship, a relationship to a person. That's what Jesus invites us to — to walk with him in service, to talk with him in prayer, [to dine with him in his Supper], to be his own and find rest for our souls.

That's a most promising invitation ... from the Lord of heaven and earth himself ... for you. Amen.

Proper 10
Pentecost 8
Ordinary Time 15
Matthew 13:1-9, 18-23 (C, L)
Matthew 13:1-23 (RC)

The Spreading Word

Jesus told them a parable: Listen up, folks. A farmer went out to plant. This was many centuries ago, before modern machinery. He carried a large bag of seeds and threw them all around by hand. In those days, a farmer threw the seeds (or "sowed" them) *before* he plowed them under. He would come along later and turn ground over so that the seeds would be covered with soil and could grow. Therefore, he wasn't so worried where he sowed them at this point. But, of course, some of the seeds fell on the path and the birds gobbled them up right away. Other seeds fell on rocky ground which really didn't get plowed well enough for the seeds to take root. Still others fell in the thorns which continued to grow and choked off the growth of those seeds. Most of the seeds, though, fell on good ground and grew into grain and there was a great harvest. Then Jesus ends very abruptly: "Let anyone with ears listen!"

Most of us have heard this story before and we know that the seed is the Christian message, the word of God, the gospel. And we know that the seed, the word, gets a different reception from different people: it just bounces off some; it just goes in one ear and out the other with others but doesn't take root; and with still others the word gets choked by all the other things in life in which they are caught up. Yet for some — indeed, for many — the word is joyfully received, takes root and bears fruit.

The parable is about God sowing the word in Jesus' own ministry. But the early church, especially when it left its familiar Old Testament context as the mission went beyond converts from Judaism to the Gentile world, didn't really know what to do with parables. Instead of seeing them as a vivid story with a clear main point, they tended to treat them instead as *allegories*, which were stories that supposedly contained hidden meanings behind each little detail. (Some Christians today still treat the Bible that way when they claim to find the explanation to current events in the book of Revelation, for example.) Most scholars think this shift to allegorical interpretation had already happened for this parable by the time Matthew's gospel was written down, perhaps a half-century after Jesus' death but certainly after the time that Christianity had become largely a movement beyond Judaism.

So the interpretation attributed to Jesus in verses 18-23 focuses on each little detail not of the seed but of the soil! And you've heard sermons like that, haven't you? What kind of soil should you be? Not hard soil, like the path, where the word doesn't sink in. Not rocky ground, which welcomes the word but doesn't allow it to take root. Not someone so absorbed in the cares of the world that the word gets choked. Don't be like that, these sermons continue; be good soil! Be people who believe the word, who study it, who take it seriously, and live it.

Now, you ask, what's wrong with that? What's wrong is that this is not what Jesus' original parable was about. The focus is no longer on the sower and the seed, on God and the word, but on ourselves. What kind of person am I? Am I the right kind; do I make the right response? Am I sincere; are my motives correct? And a secondary focus is on other people: look at them — rocky, thorny, hard — I'm glad I'm not like them.

In the original parable the focus is on the sower who spreads the seeds around with such liberality that no ground is missed. So what if a small amount of seed is wasted? The point is to cover the ground. Even today, with our more sophisticated planting machinery, we must waste a little at the ends and the corners of fields and overlap a little to make sure all the ground is covered. The picture that Jesus paints is of the sower's liberality, his generosity. The seed is going all over the place; the word is for everyone. "Let anyone with ears [that's everyone, presumably] listen." The focus is on the generosity of the one who gives the word of the kingdom to all people. The focus is on God, who sent Jesus Christ, who is God's word. You've got ears: listen to him. And the promise is that this word will bring forth a huge harvest.[2]

There is a great old hymn that appears in numerous hymnals, in a variety of translations and with different numbers of verses. It is usually known by its first words, "Spread, O Spread, Thou Mighty Word" (original German texts by Jonathan Friedrich Bahnmaier, 1774-1841). It is almost automatic, I think, that when we hear those first words, especially in more recent translations that avoid "Thou," and render it "Spread, Oh, Spread, Almighty Word,"[3] that we hear these words as a command to *us* to spread God's word. But the hymn itself portrays the word as spreading of its own power. The subject of the hymn (the actor!) is the Lord of the harvest, whose word conveys the whole trinitarian activity of the God of the Bible.

In many ways this hymn offers a more accurate interpretation of the parable of the sower than does the so-called interpretation in the thirteenth chapter of Matthew (vv. 18-23). Many other Christian hymns about God's word capture this same point: that the living, active word of God itself is the focus of the Christian gospel. This is what needs to be emphasized rather than the particulars of our human response. Hymns such as "Thy Word, O Lord, Like Gentle Dews" (Carl Bernhard Garve, 1763-1841), "Almighty God, Thy Word Is Cast" (John Cawood, 1775-1852) and "Thy Strong Word" (Martin Franzmann, 1907-1976) convey the same insight.

The initiative is with God. Sin is being turned in on ourselves; what is needed is for God to come and turn us out again and that happens as the word of Christ comes to us. Then we not only see God but we see God's world and our fellow creatures. If we focus first on our response, on what kind of soil we are, we remain turned in on ourselves. Then we domesticate Jesus, we "miniaturize" him (as someone has said), to make his word fit into our ways instead of using our ears to hear him and be pulled outside of our preoccupation with ourselves.

There is a helpful clue in our gospel reading itself, which we have skipped over until now. It starts out (13:1), *"That same day"* Jesus went down by the sea and told this parable. What same day? The day that had just been described in the twelfth chapter of Matthew. And what a day it was! It began by having Jesus' disciples pick grain on the sabbath, breaking this most sacred religious law about resting on the sabbath. Jesus got into a big argument about this with his critics and ended by declaring himself to be the Lord of the sabbath. Then he seemed to flaunt his position by arguing with the leaders of the synagogue and making them so mad they conspired to destroy him. Next, he himself did some work on that sabbath, healing all sorts of people, including one possessed of a demon. For this, his enemies denounced him as an agent of the devil. To which Jesus replied that because they don't recognize the Holy Spirit's work in his works that they are guilty of the unforgivable sin.

Then, to make things worse, Jesus promised they will be condemned — and remember, he was denouncing the "good" people of his day: the Rotarians, the Jaycees, the League of Women Voters, whom he calls "an evil and adulterous generation." Finally, to top it all off, chapter 12 ends just prior to the parable of the sower with Jesus' mother Mary and his brothers coming to see him and he dismissed them: "Who is my mother, and who are my brothers? . . . Whoever does the will of my Father in heaven is my brother and sister and mother."

Good grief! This guy is God's word? Does God's word create this sort of confusion and hatred and bitterness? "Let anyone with ears listen!" No wonder many did not respond. We shouldn't be surprised. Just a few chapters earlier Jesus had said, "Do not think that I have come to bring peace to the earth; I have not come to bring peace, but a sword" (10:34). And we know that the early church referred to the word as being sharper than any two-edged sword (Hebrews 4:12). God's word in Jesus not only cuts us free from sin but also pierces us, judges us, and lays us bare. Because we are caught in sin God's word stands in opposition to us in some important ways.

The image of the word as a seed already hints at this. The seed must be buried and die before it can bear fruit. (Compare John 12:23-26 as well as Matthew 10:37-39 and 16:24-26.) This figure describes both Christ as God's word and the resulting life of the believer. The death of the old, sinful self is part of the great harvest; only the seed that dies bears fruit. Those who want to hang on to their lives lose them but those who lose them for Christ's sake find true life (Matthew 16:25).

When we listen to Jesus our lives get rearranged. And that's good. That's what we need, whether we know it or not. The word of God will do to us what God needs done. It will build us up and encourage us; or, if we are arrogant, it will humble us. It can cut away our chains and bad habits or it can cut us down to size.

The Sower sows the word through the reading of scripture and the witness of Christians, through hymns and creeds, through sermons and sacraments (visible words!), through symbol and picture. It comes to us from outside ourselves, as a gift. God gave us all ears and graciously made it so we can't close them so that we can be saved by his word. As you hear it, know that God has come to you. Amen.

Proper 11
Pentecost 9
Ordinary Time 16
Matthew 13:24-30, 36-43 (C)
Matthew 13:24-30 (36-43) (L)
Matthew 13:24-43 (RC)

The Wheat Among The Weeds

Our gospel passage today is this peculiar parable of Jesus about the wheat and the weeds. Jesus says that the kingdom of heaven (that is, the rule of God) is like this: A man went out in his field and sowed (by hand, of course, in those days) the good seed that he had saved from the previous year's crop. It was sown all over, not in neat rows or spaced evenly. And since nearly 2,000 years ago there were no chemical fertilizers or insecticides, weeds grew up with the wheat: worthless weeds that competed for the soil's moisture and nutrients — the work of an enemy of the farmer as well as his crop.

While it is not obvious in English, the biblical word that Jesus uses for this particular weed describes an especially noxious weed that yet looks a lot like wheat at first, so that both the weed and the wheat must grow for some time before one can be certain which shoots are weeds. That's why, when the farmer's servants come and ask if they should pull up the weeds, the farmer says, "No, because they've been growing together so long that their roots are intertwined so that in pulling up the weeds you would pull up most of the wheat, too. Let them grow together until the harvest, when everything has to be pulled up anyway. Then we'll use the weeds for fuel and save the wheat in the storage barn."

If we can put ourselves back into a pre-modern mindset, we can understand this sort of common-sense story in terms of farming. But Jesus took this familiar picture and used it to talk about the rule of *God*. So, if we are to understand this parable as God's word for today, we have to see that the farmer's words and actions are those of God and the wheat and the weeds describe people in the world.

If we are Christians, if we are God's people, then we are the wheat, planted from the good seed (In baptism! See Romans 6:5, where the word translated "united" is literally "planted" with Christ in death by baptism), but living right next to, surrounded by, noxious weeds that threaten to choke us off. Christians are here portrayed as a minority in a hostile world. So, when we hear the words of Jesus to let both the weeds and the wheat grow together, that's not good news. We want our vindication— our salvation — to come sooner.

But, how do we even know for sure that we are wheat? Can we be so certain that if the weeds were pulled up, if sinners were to be gathered and thrown away right now, we wouldn't be doomed? In that case, the farmer's word to let the weed and the wheat grow together would be good news, allowing time for repentance.

Or, even if we can rightly say that we believe in Jesus, that we have been baptized into his church and saved by his blood, that we are wheat, in other words — even then, pulling up the weeds jeopardizes the wheat. Getting rid of people who don't seem to be Christians might in fact get rid of some Christians at the same time. Maybe for us Jesus' words about letting the wheat and the weeds grow together until the harvest are wise and good words. You cannot really tell which is which until the end.

There are several obvious implications of all this. God is patient; we should not judge too soon. Salvation is by grace through faith, not by accomplishments. Righteousness is not visible; God's ways and ours are not necessarily the same. Jesus is portrayed over and over in the New Testament as reaching out to all sorts of people: tax collectors, lepers, foreigners, all those called "least." Our task is to go and make disciples, to proclaim the gospel to all people, not to sit in judgment over those who are not like us.

This is hard to manage sometimes. We want to know now, especially about ourselves. We who are faithful want vindication now because we fear we might lose faith — especially as Christians become more and more of a minority. But the parable tells us that God doesn't judge now, lest in gathering up the weeds the wheat might get rooted up, too.

Let's try a more modern example. In World War II Hitler's army overran France and established a Nazi government there that virtually wiped out any sort of French nation or government. There was a French government in exile in England, but in France itself there was only a small group of people in the resistance. They were a hopeless and nearly powerless minority, praying for help, but the answer seemed always to be "No." What should they do? Would there ever be a France again? Should they still be loyal, should they still cling to their own nation?

Their struggle both as resistance fighters and in wondering what in the world the outcome would be went on for several years. Finally, this modern-day parable was worked out by force. The Allied armies liberated France and drove the Nazis into retreat and eventual surrender. And as this happened, the faithful were seen! The members of the resistance who had not cooperated with the Nazis rose up. And others of less faith or courage followed these loyalists, so France could be reestablished.

Of course, this is a secular example, but that is exactly what Jesus was using also. Perhaps we can see ourselves, members of Christ's church, as those who now need to struggle to remain faithful so that others too may see our faith and take heart. If people see only atheism and evil in the world, they will despair. Cynicism can be contagious; but so can faith and hope. God needs us as a faithful minority for the sake of the world.

We live by faith now, in any case, not by sight. We cannot know with certainty now either about our own righteousness or that of others. We live now by faith in the word of God and by hope in God's promises. We expect that God will keep the promise made in Jesus: let all grow together and at the harvest the wheat will be gathered into the safety of God's shelter. This faith and hope — and the prayer, witness and works of love that issue from them — bear witness to our true citizenship, much like the witness of those members of the French resistance movement.

(This modern parable also helps to shift our understanding away from the focus on evil weeds in the midst of the good wheat — primarily a defensive way of looking at the mission of the church — to emphasizing the presence of the wheat in the midst of the weeds — possibly a more positive way of interpreting the present struggles of the church. Hence the title of the sermon, "The Wheat Among The Weeds" rather than the other way around.)

Such an outlook on life will permeate the way we approach each day. We will stay rooted in the soil of daily life, in our roles and duties as members of families and communities, as students and homemakers, as workers and retired persons, as citizens and taxpayers, as friends and neighbors and as church members. All this contributes to the harvest that God is preparing. God is patient, to allow more people to believe. Through us who believe God may work to reach those on the edges of faith, with whom our roots intertwine, so that they may hear God's call.

This is not a matter of superiority or pride for us, certainly, nor is it to be considered a burden placed on us by God. But just as God worked through the small nation of Israel and then through one man who was crucified, so now God works even through the church, even through us. In ourselves we are not rich or powerful or famous. No, as the apostle Paul writes, we are weak; we don't even know how to pray. But the Holy Spirit intercedes for us and helps us to pray and to do God's will (Romans 8:26).

Those whom God calls God also equips. Today, we are given the good word telling us that it is God's will that the wheat and the weeds grow together, so that all the wheat will be saved. [And we also get God's word made concrete and visible in the Lord's supper. Here the grains of wheat are formed into bread and with the word are Christ's body for us. And the wine from God's grapes with the word is Christ's blood for us. This is not the heavenly banquet yet, but a foretaste of the things to come. But it is a foretaste, it is a preview of the final invasion of God's liberating rule. As we eat this bread and drink this cup, we proclaim Christ's death until he comes again (1 Corinthians 11:26)].

In this way God builds us up in faith and hope, so that we might endure, and as we endure, others also may take courage and keep growing alongside until the harvest. For as it is written in 2 Peter 3:9: "The Lord is not slow about his promise, as some think of slowness, but is patient with you, not wanting any to perish, but all to come to repentance." Thanks be to God! Amen.

Notes

1. For a classic sermon on this passage, to which I am indebted but whose profundity I cannot come close to matching, see Paul Tillich, "The Yoke of Religion," in *The Shaking Of The Foundation* (New York: Charles Scribner's Sons, 1948), pp. 93-103.

2. When this parable is interpreted with a focus on the soil, on ourselves and on how we should be, it functions as law; that is, it demands something from us and accuses us when we do not meet the demands. Law, in this sense, has many uses, including ordering our behavior in this life, but it does not save us. If the parable is interpreted in this way (as law), it is not about the kingdom of heaven — but that is supposed to be what all of Jesus' parables are about.

When the parable is interpreted with the focus on the sower and the seed rather than the soil, we can see the emphasis on God as the actor and on God's gracious liberality in sending the word (Jesus Christ) for everyone. Then the parable is gospel — "good news" of what God has done, is doing, and will do. This is just the opposite of a demand: it is a gift, it is a promise, to which the only appropriate response is faith, faith as *trust* (not as belief, which might be understood as our accomplishment, our work — a response appropriate to the law).

If we preach from faith to faith (or for faith), then only the gospel can accomplish our purposes. This is not to say that we cannot also preach about conduct or social justice — but these things are a matter of law for the good of our neighbor in this life; they are not the means of our salvation or of our right relation to God. This may be stated in another way as follows: To preach the gospel, whatever you talk about, do so in such a way that the justification (or right relationship with God) that your words open to your hearers is the justification that faith receives rather than the justification that works achieve. [See Eric Gritsch and Robert Jenson, *Lutheranism* (Philadelphia: Fortress, 1976), chapter 3.]

3. See, for example, *Lutheran Book Of Worship* (Minneapolis: Augsburg Fortress, 1978), Hymn 379.

Lectionary Preaching After Pentecost

Virtually all pastors who make use of the sermons in this book will find their worship life and planning shaped by one of two lectionary series. Most mainline Protestant denominations, along with clergy of the Roman Catholic Church, have now approved — either for provisional or official use — the three-year Revised Common (Consensus) Lectionary. This family of denominations includes United Methodist, Presbyterian, United Church of Christ and Disciples of Christ.

Lutherans and Roman Catholics, while testing the Revised Common Lectionary on a limited basis at present, follow their own three-year cycle of texts. While there are divergences between the Revised Common and Lutheran/Roman Catholic systems, the gospel texts show striking parallels, with few text selections evidencing significant differences. Nearly all the gospel texts included in this book will, therefore, be applicable to worship and preaching planning for clergy following either lectionary.

A significant divergence does occur, however, in the method by which specific gospel texts are assigned to specific calendar days. The Revised Common and Roman Catholic Lectionaries accomplish this by counting backwards from Christ the King (Last Sunday after Pentecost), discarding "extra" texts from the front of the list: Lutherans follow the opposite pattern, counting forward from The Holy Trinity, discarding "extra" texts at the end of the list.

The following index will aid the user of this book in matching the correct text to the correct Sunday during the Pentecost portion of the church year.

(Fixed dates do not pertain to Lutheran Lectionary)

Fixed Date Lectionaries *Revised Common and Roman Catholic*	**Lutheran Lectionary** *Lutheran*
The Day of Pentecost	The Day of Pentecost
The Holy Trinity	The Holy Trinity
May 29-June 4 — Proper 4, Ordinary Time 9	Pentecost 2
June 5-11 — Proper 5, Ordinary Time 10	Pentecost 3
June 12-18 — Proper 6, Ordinary Time 11	Pentecost 4
June 19-25 — Proper 7, Ordinary Time 12	Pentecost 5
June 26-July 2 — Proper 8, Ordinary Time 13	Pentecost 6

July 3-9 — Proper 9, Ordinary Time 14	Pentecost 7
July 10-16 — Proper 10, Ordinary Time 15	Pentecost 8
July 17-23 — Proper 11, Ordinary Time 16	Pentecost 9
July 24-30 — Proper 12, Ordinary Time 17	Pentecost 10
July 31-Aug. 6 — Proper 13, Ordinary Time 18	Pentecost 11
Aug. 7-13 — Proper 14, Ordinary Time 19	Pentecost 12
Aug. 14-20 — Proper 15, Ordinary Time 20	Pentecost 13
Aug. 21-27 — Proper 16, Ordinary Time 21	Pentecost 14
Aug. 28-Sept. 3 — Proper 17, Ordinary Time 22	Pentecost 15
Sept. 4-10 — Proper 18, Ordinary Time 23	Pentecost 16
Sept. 11-17 — Proper 19, Ordinary Time 24	Pentecost 17
Sept. 18-24 — Proper 20, Ordinary Time 25	Pentecost 18
Sept. 25-Oct. 1 — Proper 21, Ordinary Time 26	Pentecost 19
Oct. 2-8 — Proper 22, Ordinary Time 27	Pentecost 20
Oct. 9-15 — Proper 23, Ordinary Time 28	Pentecost 21
Oct. 16-22 — Proper 24, Ordinary Time 29	Pentecost 22
Oct. 23-29 — Proper 25, Ordinary Time 30	Pentecost 23
Oct. 30-Nov. 5 — Proper 26, Ordinary Time 31	Pentecost 24
Nov. 6-12 — Proper 27, Ordinary Time 32	Pentecost 25
Nov. 13-19 — Proper 28, Ordinary Time 33	Pentecost 26 Pentecost 27
Nov. 20-26 — Christ the King	Christ the King

Reformation Day (or last Sunday in October) is October 31 (Revised Common, Lutheran)

All Saints' Day (or first Sunday in November) is November 1 (Revised Common, Lutheran, Roman Catholic)

Books In This Cycle A Series

Gospel Set

God In Flesh Made Manifest
Sermons For Advent, Christmas And Epiphany
Mark Radecke

Whispering The Lyrics
Sermons For Lent And Easter
Thomas Long

Christ Our Sure Foundation
Sermons For Pentecost (First Third)
Marc Kolden

Good News For The Hard Of Hearing
Sermons For Pentecost (Middle Third)
Roger G. Talbott

Invitations To The Light
Sermons For Pentecost (Last Third)
Phyllis Faaborg Wolkenhauer

First Lesson Set

Hope Beneath The Surface
Sermons For Advent, Christmas And Epiphany
Paul E. Robinson

Caught In The Acts
Sermons For Lent And Easter
Ed Whetstone

Tenders Of The Sacred Fire
Sermons For Pentecost (First Third)
Robert Cueni

What Do You Say To A Burning Bush?
Sermons For Pentecost (Middle Third)
Steven E. Burt

Veiled Glimpses Of God's Glory
Sermons For Pentecost (Last Third)
Robert S. Crilley

Second Lesson Set

Empowered By The Light
Sermons For Advent, Christmas And Epiphany
Richard A. Hasler

Ambassadors Of Hope
Sermons For Lent And Easter
Sandra Hefter Herrmann